DISCARD

WEST GEORGIA REGIONAL LIBRARY SYSTEM
Neva Lomason Memorial Library

**Georgia, My State
Native Americans**

Creeks and Cherokees Today
Book 7

by Jill Ward

Your State • Your Standards • Your Grade Level

Dear Educators, Librarians and Parents . . .

Thank you for choosing the *"Georgia, My State"* Series! We have designed this series to support the Georgia Department of Education's Georgia Performance Standards for elementary level Georgia studies. Each book in the series has been written at appropriate grade level as measured by the ATOS Readability Formula for Books (Accelerated Reader), the Lexile Framework for Reading, and the Fountas & Pinnell Benchmark Assessment System for Guided Reading. Photographs and/or illustrations, captions, and other design elements have been included to provide supportive visual messaging to enhance text comprehension. Glossary and Word Index sections introduce key new words and help young readers develop skills in locating and combining information.

We wish you all success in using the *"Georgia, My State"* Series to meet your student or child's learning needs. For additional sources of information, see www.georgiaencyclopedia.org.

Jill Ward, President

Publisher
State Standards Publishing, LLC
1788 Quail Hollow
Hamilton, GA 31811
USA
1.866.740.3056
www.statestandardspublishing.com

Library of Congress Cataloging-in-Publication Data
Ward, Jill, 1952-
  Creeks and Cherokees today / by Jill Ward.
      p. cm. -- (Georgia, my state. Native Americans ; book 7)
  ISBN-13: 978-1-935077-80-0 (hardcover)
  ISBN-10: 1-935077-80-5 (hardcover)
  ISBN-13: 978-1-935077-87-9 (pbk.)
  ISBN-10: 1-935077-87-2 (pbk.)
  1. Creek Indians--Georgia--Juvenile literature. 2. Cherokee Indians--Georgia--Juvenile literature. 3. Georgia--Ethnic relations--Juvenile literature. I. Title.
  E99.C9W38 2010
  975.004'97385--dc22
                                                                  2010005906

Copyright © 2010 by State Standards Publishing, LLC. All rights reserved. No part of this book may be reproduced, stored, or transmitted in any form or by any means without prior written permission from the publisher.

Printed in the United States of America, North Mankato, Minnesota, March 2010, 120209.

About the Author

Jill Ward has more than twenty years' experience as a creative writer for business and organization promotional and educational needs, including video scripts, brochures, marketing and educational materials, white papers, and feature articles. She is the founder and president of State Standards Publishing and lives in Georgia with her husband, Harry.

Table of Contents

The Trail of Tears 5
Creek Tribes Today 7
Cherokee Tribes Today 11
American Citizens 15
Remembering Traditions 17
Glossary 22
Word Index 23
Time Line 24

Cherokees called the journey the *Trail of Tears*.

The Trail of Tears

The Creeks and Cherokees lived in Georgia until the 1830s. Many **settlers** came to America. They came to build homes. They wanted the new land. The Creeks, Cherokees, and other Indians had to move to Oklahoma. The Cherokees called the journey the *Trail of Tears*.

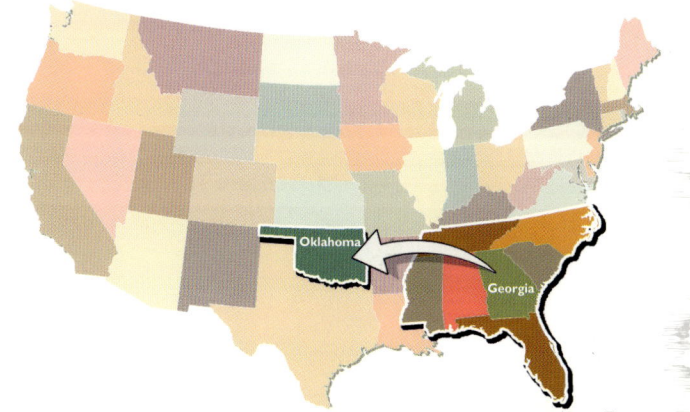

Chief A.D. Ellis

Oklahoma

Muscogee Creek Nation → Okmulgee

Chief A. D. Ellis meets with President George Bush. Chief Ellis is Principal Chief of the Muscogee Creek Nation.

Creek Tribes Today

Today, there are two Creek **tribes**, or groups of Native Americans. The largest tribe is the **Muscogee Creek Nation**. Its capital is Okmulgee, Oklahoma. The tribe is led by a **principal chief.** A **council** makes laws for the tribe. Men and women are **elected** to the council. Tribe members **vote** for them. They choose people for the council.

Appalachian Plateau

Blue Ridge Mountains

Valley and Ridge

Alabama

Piedmont

Georgia

Poarch Creek
Indian Reservation
★ Poarch
★ Atmore

Upper Coastal Plain

Lower Coastal Plain

Poarch Creek Indian land is a reservation.

The **Poarch Band of Creek Indians** is in Alabama. They are the only Creeks who did not move to Oklahoma. Poarch Creek Indian land is a **reservation**. This is land that belongs to the tribe. They are led by a chief and a council, too. Their chief is called a **chairman**.

Chad "Corntassel" Smith is Principal Chief of the Cherokee Nation.

The Cherokee Nation is in Oklahoma.

10

Cherokee Tribes Today

There are three Cherokee tribes today. The largest tribe is the **Cherokee Nation**. Its capital is Tahlequah, Oklahoma. The **United Keetoowah Band of Cherokees** is also in Oklahoma. These tribes are led by a principal chief. A council makes laws for the tribe. Men and women are elected to the council.

The Eastern Band of Cherokee Indians stayed in North Carolina.

Some Cherokees also belong to the **Eastern Band of Cherokee Indians**. Its capital is Cherokee, North Carolina. These Cherokees did not go to Oklahoma. They are led by a chief and a council, like other Cherokees and Creeks.

Native Americans live and work all over America.

Creeks and Cherokees are citizens, like this girl.

Creeks and Cherokees have all the rights of other Americans.

14

American Citizens

Today, Creeks and Cherokees are **citizens**. They have all the rights of other Americans, like voting. They speak English and other languages. They live and work all over America. They wear the same clothes other Americans do. But they are still **Native Americans**! They were the first type of people to live in America!

Some Cherokees speak and write the Cherokee language.

Remembering Traditions

Creeks and Cherokees also remember their **traditions**. They remember the ways their **ancestors** lived. Ancestors are relatives from a long time ago. Some Creeks still speak the Muscogee language. Some Cherokees speak and write the Cherokee language.

Making Baskets

Carving a Mask

Telling Stories

Native Americans enjoy arts and crafts.

Many Native Americans enjoy **arts and crafts**. Creeks and Cherokees do, too! They make things like their ancestors did. They make baskets. They weave cloth. They make bows and arrows. They carve masks out of wood. Some paint or write about the ways of their ancestors. Some tell stories.

Singing

Dancing

Native Americans hold pow-wows.

Many Native Americans hold **pow-wows**. Creeks and Cherokees hold pow-wows, too. A pow-wow is like a ceremony or a meeting. The people tell stories. They sing songs and dance. They show their arts and crafts. This helps them remember that they were America's first people!

Arts and Crafts

Glossary

ancestors – Relatives from a long time ago.

arts and crafts – Things Native Americans make like their ancestors did.

chairman – The leader of a tribe, like a chief.

Cherokee Nation – The largest tribe of Cherokee Indians.

citizens – People who belong to a city, state, or country and have rights, like voting.

council – A group of people that makes laws for a tribe.

Eastern Band of Cherokees – A Cherokee tribe in North Carolina.

elected – To be chosen by voting.

Muscogee Creek Nation – The largest tribe of Creek Indians.

Native Americans – The first type of people to live in America.

Poarch Band of Creek Indians – A Creek tribe in Alabama.

pow-wows – Ceremonies or meetings of Native Americans.

principal chief – The leader of a Creek or Cherokee tribe today.

reservation – Land that belongs to a tribe.

settlers – People who build homes in a new land.

traditions – The ways ancestors lived.

tribes – Groups of Native Americans.

United Keetoowah Band of Cherokees – A tribe of Cherokees in Oklahoma.

vote – To choose a person for a job, like serving on a council.

Word Index

Alabama, 9
America, Americans, 5, 15, 21
ancestors, 17, 19
arts and crafts, 19, 21
chairman, 9
Cherokee Nation, 11
chief, 9, 13
citizens, 15
clothes, 15
council, 7, 9, 11, 13
Eastern Band of Cherokee Indians, 13

elected, 7, 11
Georgia, 5
land, 5, 9
language, languages, 15, 17
laws, 7, 11
move, 5, 9
Muscogee Creek Nation, 7
Native Americans, 15, 19, 21
North Carolina, 13
Oklahoma, 5, 7, 9, 11, 13
Poarch Band of Creek Indians, 9

pow-wows, 21
principal chief, 7, 11
reservation, 9
rights, 15
settlers, 5
traditions, 17
Trail of Tears, 5
tribe, tribes, 7, 9, 11
United Keetoowah Band of Cherokees, 11
vote, voting, 7, 15
work, 15

Image Credits

Cover Principal Chief: © Phil Konstantin, http://americanindian.net/kusi.html
p. 4 "Trail of Tears" painting by Troy Anderson, © Marilyn Angel Wynn, NativeStock.com
p. 5 US map: © John Woodcock, iStockphoto.com
p. 6 Chief and President: © Bloomberg via Getty Images
p. 8 Reservation sign: © Emile Mattison (Ute/Shoshone)
p. 10 Cherokee Nation sign: © Marilyn Angel Wynn, NativeStock.com; Principal Chief: © Phil Konstantin, http://americanindian.net/kusi.html
p. 12 Eastern Band of Cherokees: © Marilyn Angel Wynn, NativeStock.com
p. 14 Ceremonial flag: © Joeygil/Dreamstime.com; Girl with flag: © Marilyn Angel Wynn, NativeStock.com; Man with phone: © Mona Makela, iStockphoto.com
p. 16 Street sign: © Marilyn Angel Wynn, NativeStock.com
p. 18 Basket maker: © Marilyn Angel Wynn, NativeStock.com; Mask carver: © Marilyn Angel Wynn, NativeStock.com; Storyteller: © Marilyn Angel Wynn, NativeStock.com
p. 20 Dancer: © Emile Mattison (Ute/Shoshone); Singer: © Emile Mattison (Ute/Shoshone)
p. 21 Arts and crafts: © Marilyn Angel Wynn, NativeStock.com
p. 24 Woodland Indian: © Buddy Mays, Travel Stock Photography, buddymays.com; All other images: © Marilyn Angel Wynn, NativeStock.com

Editorial Credits

Designer: Michael Sellner, Corporate Graphics, North Mankato, Minnesota

Native Americans Time Line

Paleo-Indians

Woodland Indians

Shell Mound Builders

Mississippian Indians

Creeks

Cherokees

Creeks and Cherokees Today

24

```
WGRL-HQ   JUV
31057100725400
J 970. 1973 WARD
Ward, Jill
Creeks and Cherokees today
```